Usborne Spotter's Guides
WEATHER

Designed by Candice Whatmore and Ruth Russell
Illustrated by Verinder Bhachu, Gary Bines, Kuo Kang Chen, David Wright
Edited by Judy Tatchell
Cover designer: Michael Hill
Series designer: Laura Fearn
Consultants: Roger Trend and Francis Wilson
With thanks to Malcolm Walker (Royal Meteorological Society)

Acknowledgements: Cover, © Getty Images/Don Farrall; ©R.K. Pilsbury
FRPS (Royal Meteorological Society Collection) p.4, p.12 (tr), (ml), p.13,
p.22, p.23, p.24-25 (background), p.24, p.25 (ml), (bl), p.26, p.27, p.28. p.29,
p.46 (l); Corbis p.18-19 (background) ©Galen Rowell/CORBIS, p.52-53
(background) ©Bettmann/CORBIS; ©CORBIS Digital Stock p.6-7, p.30-31
(background), p.32-33 (background), p.50-51; © Royalty-Free/CORBIS,
p.2-3 (background); ©Digital Vision p.1, p.10 (tr), p.10-11 (background), p.11
(tl), (tm), p.12 (br), p.12-13 (background), p.22-23 (background), p.26-27
(background), p.28-29 (background), p.36-37 (background), p.40-41
(background), p.40, p.41 (main), p.44-45 (background); ©National
Oceanic and Atmospheric Administration (NOAA)/Dept. of Commerce
p.8-9 (background), p.25 (tr), p.46 (m), (r), p.47, p.55(tr), p.56 (t); ©NOAA/
National Climatic Data Center p.57 (br); ©NOAA/Satellite Services Division
p.57(tr); ©NOAA/National Severe Storms Laboratory p.54-55
(background), p.55(ml); ©Chris Kridler p.55 (br); Information to create
the synoptic chart, p.58, and the weather map, p.60, was supplied by
the Met Office.

This edition first published in 2006 by Usborne Publishing Ltd.,
Usborne House, 83-85 Saffron Hill, London, EC1N 8RT, England.
www.usborne.com

Copyright © 2006, 2001, 1979 Usborne Publishing Ltd.
The name Usborne and the devices ♀ 🎈 are Trade Marks
of Usborne Publishing Ltd.

Printed in China

CONTENTS

HOW TO USE THIS BOOK

This book gives you a general introduction to weather. It explains the basic elements that cause all sorts of different conditions: the atmosphere, the Sun's energy, and the Earth's water. Then it explains how these elements produce different types of weather, and helps you to spot them for yourself.

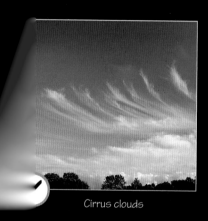

Cirrus clouds

← WEATHER SPOTTING
In this book you will come across some pages of photographs showing different weather features, mainly types of cloud. Next to each photo is a circle to tick when you have seen the feature. Look at pages 12-13 and pages 22-29 for these photographic guides.

WEATHER WEBSITES
On page 61, you'll find a list of websites relating to weather and weather organizations. The World Wide Web is a great resource for weather spotters. You can find weather forecasts from all around the world, as well as satellite images and detailed meteorology (weather science) sites.

WEATHER WORDS
As you read this book, you may find some unfamiliar words relating to weather and weather science. Most of these words are explained in the place where they first occur in the book. You can also look them up in the glossary of weather terms and other useful words on page 62.

Throughout this book, you will find suggested links to websites.
For a complete list of links and instructions, turn to page 61.

THE ATMOSPHERE

The Earth is covered in a blanket of air called the atmosphere. This is held in place by gravity, and is kept swirling around by heat that the Earth receives from the Sun. The atmosphere is divided into layers according to temperature.

■ **Thermosphere** Contains gases which absorb some of the Sun's harmful radiation. This heats the layer up to 1500 C at its upper limit (about 450km). Above that is a layer containing very few gases which merges into space at about 1000km.

■ **Mesosphere** Contains few gases and is completely dry. This makes it very cold.

□ **Stratosphere** Contains a layer of ozone gas which absorbs most of the Sun's harmful ultraviolet radiation. Because of this, the stratosphere is warm towards its upper limit.

□ **Troposphere** This is where all of the Earth's weather happens. It is the only layer with enough water vapour to form clouds. Where the troposphere meets the stratosphere is called the tropopause.

Space Shuttle orbits in the thermosphere

Thermosphere

80km

Meteors burn up here

Mesosphere

50km

Stratosphere

Ozone layer

15km Tropopause

Troposphere

Sea level

SUNLIGHT

The Sun sends out a constant supply of energy called radiation, which provides the Earth with heat and light. This picture shows what happens when the radiation reaches Earth.

Radiation from Sun

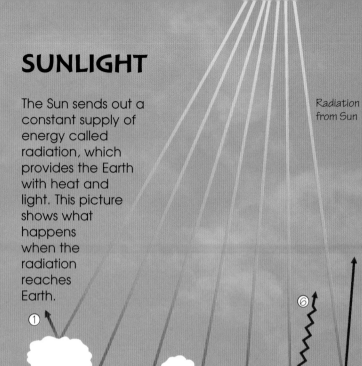

① Some radiation is reflected back into space by clouds.

② The highest intensity radiation is absorbed by the Earth.

③ A lot of the radiation is deflected to Earth by clouds.

④ Radiation warms Earth, which gives off heat, warming the air above.

⑤ Clouds take in heat from the Earth and reflect it back.

⑥ Some of the heat given off by Earth escapes into space.

⑦ Where there is snow, the Sun's radiation is not absorbed.

For a link to an online guide to weather with photos, turn to page 61.

TYPES OF RADIATION

The Sun gives out different types of radiation. These travel in waves of energy, which have different wavelengths.

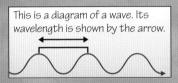

This is a diagram of a wave. Its wavelength is shown by the arrow.

• **Ultraviolet (UV) radiation**. Short wavelength. Harmful and invisible. The ozone layer absorbs most of this.

• **Visible light**. Long wavelength. Looks white, but contains all the colours of the rainbow.

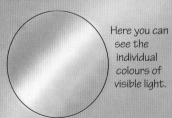

Here you can see the individual colours of visible light.

• **Infrared (IR) radiation**. Very long wavelength. Invisible. This is what you feel as heat.

SUN'S INTENSITY

The Sun's rays (its radiation) travel in straight lines. The effect on the Earth is most intense where the rays hit the Earth full-on, or almost full-on, such as near the Equator. Here they are most concentrated.

Concentrated rays – strong effect

The rays are weakest where they hit the Earth at a great angle, such as the North and South Poles. The heat is spread over a large area, so those regions don't warm up much.

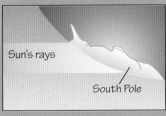

Spread-out rays – weak effect

7

BENDING SUNLIGHT

The Sun's rays look colourless, but in fact they are made up of lots of different colours. These colours can be seen when a ray is split as it passes through a raindrop in the air.

When you see a rainbow, millions of the Sun's rays are being split by millions of raindrops in the sky. Depending on its position relative to you, each drop beams a certain colour into your eye.

Inside a raindrop, the Sun's ray is split and bent. It breaks into different colours.

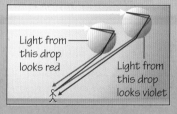

Light from this drop looks red

Light from this drop looks violet

SEEING A RAINBOW

A rainbow looks like a single, multi-coloured arch, but you are really seeing different colours from different raindrops. Each drop reflects sunlight of all colours, but only one colour reaches your eye from each drop. The colour that the drop deflects to your eye depends on its height and angle in relation to you.

Sun's rays

The visible colours range from red to violet

For a link to satellite images of recent weather events, turn to page 61.

COLOUR CHANGES

The Earth's atmosphere contains millions of tiny particles. These include the gas molecules that make air itself, plus specks of dust, salt, water and other chemicals. The Sun's rays that reach the Earth are constantly being bent and split by particles that they hit. Look out for the different colour effects that this can cause in the sky.

Midday – Sun overhead

CLEAR BLUE SKIES

On a clear day, the sky looks blue. The parts of the Sun's rays with the shortest wavelength, the blue light, is scattered in all directions. This blue light therefore travels to your eye from all directions, so the sky is blue.

Evening – Sun low in sky

RED SUNSETS

At sunset, the Sun's rays have to travel through more of the atmosphere than during the day. As a result, they bump into more air and particles of dust. The red light, though, which has the longest wavelength, easily passes through the atmosphere, so this colour reaches your eye.

WATER IN THE AIR

Water from the Earth's surface can be held in the atmosphere. It gets there by a process called evaporation.

You can see water vapour turning into droplets on a cold window

EVAPORATION

When water and the air above it are warm, the water on the surface turns into tiny, invisible particles called water vapour. This is called evaporation. The water vapour is then held in the warm air.

CONDENSATION

When air that contains water vapour is cooled, the vapour turns into droplets of water. This is called condensation. Clouds are formed as a result of water vapour in the air condensing.

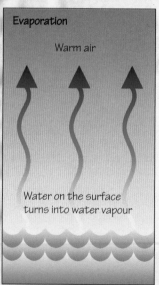

Evaporation

Warm air

Water on the surface turns into water vapour

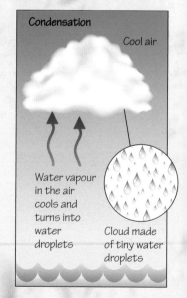

Condensation

Cool air

Water vapour in the air cools and turns into water droplets

Cloud made of tiny water droplets

DIFFERENT FORMS
In the air, water can exist in gas, liquid or solid form.

The air holds water vapour: tiny, invisible particles of gas.

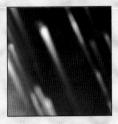

Liquid water drops, such as in clouds, mist, fog and rain.

Solid ice, such as ice crystals, hailstones, and snowflakes.

Water in the air can change from one form to another, depending on how the weather affects the temperature of the air holding it.

THE WATER CYCLE
In the atmosphere, evaporation and condensation are going on all the time, as part of a process called the water cycle. The picture below shows how it happens.

Water vapour condenses and forms clouds

Water evaporates from sea

Water falls as rain

Water in rivers flows to the sea

FOG, DEW, FROST AND RIME

Moist air cooling near the Earth's surface can create a range of conditions.

➡ FOG
When warm air flows over cold land or sea, its water vapour condenses. The result is fog. Mist is the same as fog, but less dense.

⬅ MORNING FOG
This is common in valleys. It is caused by cold mountain air moving gently downhill into valleys, particularly in the early morning. Fog evaporates quickly on sunny days, as the air temperature rises.

➡ DEW
This forms on clear nights. The ground cools quickly, cooling the air above it. Moisture in the cooling air condenses, coating objects on the ground with tiny water droplets. This is dew.

➡ FROST ON WINDOWS
On nights when the temperature dips below 0°C (freezing point), dew and tiny water droplets can freeze, forming beautiful ice-crystal patterns on cold windows.

⬅ GROUND FROST
This occurs if dew freezes. It also forms when the temperature of water vapour falls sharply to form ice crystals directly, without becoming water droplets first.

➡ RIME
A dramatic type of frost, formed in fog that is lower than 0°C. Very cold water droplets freeze when they touch objects, forming a delicate crust of white crystals.

13

AIR PRESSURE

Each square metre of the Earth's surface has about 10 tonnes of air above it. This weight exerts a force on the area beneath it, called air pressure.

DIFFERENT PRESSURES

The air pressure on the Earth's surface varies. This is partly because the Earth's surface receives different amounts of heat from the Sun. The surface releases the heat it gains into the air above, and this affects the air pressure.

Warmed air – low pressure

Air rises when warmed, leaving less pressing down on the Earth. The air pressure goes down.

Cooled air – high pressure

Air sinks when cooled. This results in more air pressing down. The air pressure rises.

High-pressure air tends to move to areas of low pressure. This moving of air on the Earth's surface is what you feel as wind. Generally, high air pressure gives dry, fair and settled weather. Low pressure gives unsettled, wet weather.

BAROMETERS

These are instruments that are designed to measure the air's pressure.

MERCURY BAROMETER

A glass tube is attached to a supply of mercury. The tube is marked with a scale.

As air pressure rises, it pushes down on the mercury, forcing it up the tube. If air pressure falls, the mercury level falls in the tube.

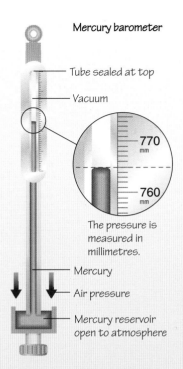

Mercury barometer

Tube sealed at top

Vacuum

770 mm

760 mm

The pressure is measured in millimetres.

Mercury

Air pressure

Mercury reservoir open to atmosphere

Aneroid barometer

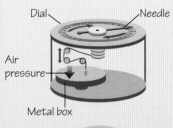

Dial

Needle

Air pressure

Metal box

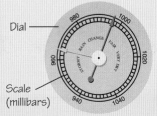

Dial

Scale (millibars)

ANEROID BAROMETER

This consists of a needle attached to a metal box that has been partly emptied of air, making a partial vacuum. If air pressure rises, the box contracts; if it falls, the box expands.

As the metal box moves in and out, the needle attached to it moves, pointing to a dial that indicates the air pressure.

15

For a link to a detailed guide to meteorology, turn to page 61.

THERMOMETERS

Weather forecasters use thermometers to measure the highest and lowest air temperatures in a certain period. They place the thermometers in the shade, so that measurements aren't affected by the Sun's direct rays.

HIGH AND LOW TEMPERATURE

Maximum thermometers measure the highest temperature reached. They contain mercury. When the temperature rises, the mercury expands and rises in the tube.

When the temperature stops rising, the mercury stops expanding. It can't fall back from the highest point, though: a tiny constriction near the tube's bulb stops it from running back.

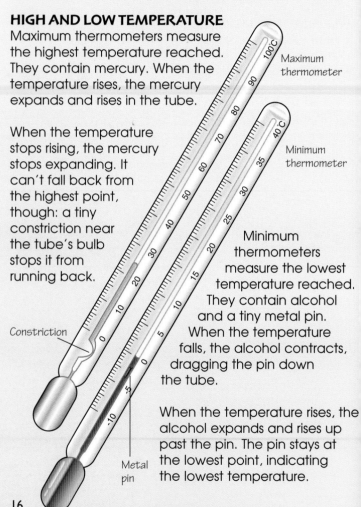

Maximum thermometer

Minimum thermometer

Constriction

Metal pin

Minimum thermometers measure the lowest temperature reached. They contain alcohol and a tiny metal pin. When the temperature falls, the alcohol contracts, dragging the pin down the tube.

When the temperature rises, the alcohol expands and rises up past the pin. The pin stays at the lowest point, indicating the lowest temperature.

HYGROMETERS

Weather forecasters use hygrometers to measure the amount of water vapour in the air.

WET BULB-DRY BULB

A common type of hygrometer consists of two thermometers. These are set up as shown in this picture.

This is called the wet bulb.

Wet cloth is wrapped around the base of the wet bulb.

A dish containing distilled water keeps the cloth wet.

This is called the dry bulb. It measures the air temperature.

HOW IT WORKS

Water evaporating from the wet cloth cools the wet bulb, so the temperature shown is lower than that on the dry bulb. If the air contains lots of water vapour, less evaporates from the cloth, so the temperature difference is smaller, indicating high humidity.

HYGROMETRIC TABLES

By using these, the difference between the two readings can be converted into a percentage – the relative humidity. The greater the difference in the readings, the drier the air (and the lower the relative humidity).

DRY BULB TEMPERATURE (°C)	DIFFERENCE BETWEEN THERMOMETER READINGS (°C)					RELATIVE HUMIDITY (%)
	0°	2.5°	5°	7°	10°	
30°	100	78	63	47	33	
10°	100	68	38	15	1	

This chart shows some examples from hygrometric tables.

17

For a link to weather forecasts around the world, turn to page 61.

CLOUDS

Clouds are made up of millions of tiny, very light water drops or particles of ice. They form when air is cooled below its dew point, or lower, and the water vapour in the air condenses onto particles of smoke, dust and salt floating in the air.

HOW CLOUDS FORM
Most clouds form as the result of convection, that is, when warm air rises through colder air.

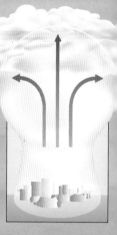

 Warm air rising

Bubble of warm air expands and rises

Cloud forms when dew point is reached

A warm patch of the Earth's surface heats the air touching it. This creates a large bubble of warm air, which is in contact with the ground.

When it is warm and large enough, the bubble rises, or convects, through the denser, colder air. As it rises, it expands and begins to cool.

When the bubble cools enough, the water vapour in the air condenses, and a cloud forms. The cooling air becomes too cold and heavy to rise further.

LAYERS OF CLOUD

Some clouds form in spread-out layers.

A rising bubble of air, already cooled below its dew point, meets a layer of warmer air.

The air bubble is trapped, creating what is known as a temperature inversion.

As air bubbles rise, they spread out below the layer of warmer air, forming layers of cloud.

LOW CLOUD

Mist and fog are simply clouds that are close to the ground. They form on clear nights when air in contact with the ground cools rapidly, becoming cooler than the air above. A temperature inversion (see above) occurs very close to the ground.

19

CLOUD CLASSIFICATION

Clouds are classified according to where in the sky they form. There are four basic types, explained here.

HIGH-LEVEL CLOUDS
These are called **cirriform**, and exist in the troposphere's highest region. They are wispy, and made of ice crystals.

MEDIUM-LEVEL CLOUDS
Called **altiform**, these grow halfway up the troposphere, forming white sheets of water drops and ice crystals.

LOW-LEVEL CLOUDS
These are called **stratiform**, and exist in the lowest part of the troposphere. They are made of water, and are thick, grey and featureless.

Cirrocumulus are cirriform clouds. They are individual clouds of ice crystals. You might see them arranged in a row, as here.

Altocumulus clouds are altiform. Made of small, grey or white cumulus clouds of similar size, they often lie in rows, and are sometimes joined together, as here.

Cirrostratus clouds are cirriform clouds that form a thin, near-transparent layer over the whole sky. They often bring rain.

Stratus clouds are stratiform. They sit in a layer across the sky, often producing rain or drizzle.

Stratocumulus clouds are stratiform. They are a sheet of rounded cumulus clouds which are almost joined together.

For a link to a website about how to identify clouds, turn to page 61.

ALL-LEVEL CLOUDS

Clouds that exist at all levels, and often grow upwards, are called **cumuliform**. At lower levels they are made of water drops. If they push up to high levels, they contain ice crystals too. Look out for their flat bases and billowing, white tops that are often shaped like cauliflower heads.

Cumulonimbus clouds are cumuliform. They can grow to great heights, developing flat, anvil-like heads at the tropopause. When you see these watch out for heavy rain – and maybe thunder.

Cirrus clouds are cirriform. They have a feathery appearance.

Altostratus clouds are altiform, and usually make a grey sheet of cloud across the sky. You might be able to see sunlight filtering through them.

Cumulus clouds are cumuliform. They are often seen on dry, sunny days.

Nimbostratus clouds are normally stratiform. They are a thick, grey layer, with an uneven base. They bring rain.

21

HIGH-LEVEL CLOUDS

➡ CIRRUS
Wispy streaks of high-level clouds made of ice crystals. When blown by the wind, they look like strands of hair, which are sometimes referred to as "mares' tails". Cirrus clouds indicate fine weather.

⬅ CIRRUS
When there is very little wind at high levels in the sky, cirrus clouds have a rather irregular, tangled appearance.

➡ CIRROCUMULUS
This formation is often called a "mackerel sky". Cirrocumulus are high clouds that ripple across the sky in patterns like those made by wind on a sandy beach. They indicate fine weather.

➡ CIRROSTRATUS

This is a thin veil of pale, ice-crystal cloud. It can cover much or all of the sky. Cirrostratus clouds indicate changeable weather and approaching rain.

⬅ HALO

Rays of sunlight bend when they fall on the ice crystals that make up cirrostratus clouds. This creates a ring, known as a halo, around the Sun or Moon. Only cirrostratus clouds cause this effect.

➡ HALO WITH SUNDOGS

Sometimes, the bending of sunlight that causes a halo (see above) can also create brightly coloured spots in the sky, called sundogs. These appear on a level horizontal with the Sun.

MEDIUM-LEVEL CLOUDS

← ALTOSTRATUS
This is a cloud layer, like a cirrostratus cloud, but it is thicker and lower in the sky. The sky looks milky, and the Sun can just be seen. Altostratus clouds indicate approaching rain, or snow if it is cold enough.

➡ NIMBOSTRATUS
This is a thick rain cloud (*nimbus* is Latin for rain). Although sometimes classed as a medium-level cloud, as here, it often extends into high and low levels of the sky.

➡ ALTOCUMULUS
This is a thicker, lower version of cirrocumulus cloud. It looks like a layer of cotton wool. Altocumulus clouds form when bubbles of warm air rise and cool below their dew point. They indicate fine weather.

➤ ALTOCUMULUS CASTELLANUS

These are altocumulus clouds that billow upwards in rows. They can look like turreted castle walls. They can be a sign of a summer thunderstorm.

◆ ALTOCUMULUS LENTICULARIS

Air that has risen over mountains sometimes carries on blowing up and down, in waves, on the far side. These clouds form at the crest of each wave. They are rare, and can look like flying saucers.

◆ ALTOCUMULUS and ALTOSTRATUS

This picture shows altocumulus clouds merging into thick sheets of altostratus cloud. This sort of sky indicates rain or snow closing in.

LOW-LEVEL CLOUDS

➡ STRATUS
This is a thick sheet of
low-level cloud made of
water drops. If it occurs
near the ground or sea
level, it is classed as fog.
Stratus cloud usually
brings drizzle, or light
snow in winter.

⬅ STRATUS FRACTUS
This shows stratus cloud
broken up by wind,
giving a ragged
appearance.

➡ STRATOCUMULUS
This shows long, rolling
bands of stratocumulus
clouds in a summer sky.

CUMULIFORM CLOUDS

← FAIR WEATHER CUMULUS HUMILIS
These are small puffs of cloud made by rising bubbles of warm air cooling below their dew point. They often evaporate away within minutes.

→ FAIR WEATHER CUMULUS MEDIOCRIS
Medium-sized cumulus clouds, also formed by rising bubbles of warm air. Their flat bases mark the height where the air reaches its dew point and condensation begins.

← FAIR WEATHER CUMULUS CONGESTUS
A large cumulus cloud, towering up into higher levels of the sky. Unlike smaller cumulus clouds, these are large enough to produce showers.

27

CUMULIFORM CLOUDS

← CUMULONIMBUS
This is a cumulonimbus cloud over a mountain. It was formed as air was forced up over the mountain, cooling rapidly to form cloud. This type of cloud formation is called orographic formation.

→ CUMULONIMBUS
Cumulonimbus are large rain clouds that form when warm, moist air rises up into cold air. In this picture, the rain shower can be seen as a grey area underneath the cloud.

→ CUMULONIMBUS
In this picture, the rain from a cumulonimbus cloud can be seen evaporating before it reaches the ground.

➡ CUMULONIMBUS
When a cumulonimbus cloud grows high enough to reach the tropopause, its head spreads out into an anvil shape. Rain falls underneath the cloud, while hail forms in the vertical currents inside it.

⬅ CLOUD STREET
Cumulus clouds occasionally spread out and join together parallel to the direction of the wind. This formation is known as a "street" or a "line".

⬅ MAMMATUS
These are large blobs of cloud hanging down from the base of a cumulonimbus cloud, like giant udders. Mammatus clouds are a sign of strong winds and heavy rain.

29

RAIN, SNOW, HAIL, SLEET

Clouds consist of water, in the form of very tiny water droplets, ice particles or ice crystals. If these join together and become too heavy to stay in the cloud the water falls – as rain, snow, hail or sleet. Water that falls from clouds, in any form, is called precipitation.

RAIN

In warm conditions, only rain tends to occur. It forms by a process called coalescence.

Coalescence

2. As they rise, droplets bump into each other and join to form bigger drops.

1. Tiny water droplets in a cloud are blown upwards by air currents.

3. The water drops become so heavy that they fall as rain.

For a link to the UK Meteorological Office Website, turn to page 61.

SNOW

In cool conditions, clouds often stretch up into air that is below freezing. Here, they contain ice crystals and tiny droplets of water that are supercooled (still liquid but colder than freezing). A process called accretion takes place.

1. Supercooled water droplets freeze onto ice particles.

2. The increase in size leads to the formation of ice crystals.

3. Ice crystals join together to make snowflakes.

4. If the air below is cold, snow falls. If warm, the snow melts into rain.

HAIL

Hail forms in clouds containing strong up-and-down currents of air. Accretion occurs so rapidly that, instead of snow, blobs of ice form. The blobs move up and down in the cloud, becoming coated with more and more layers of ice.

Layers of ice

Cross-section of a hailstone

SLEET

Look out for sleet, which is a mixture of rain and snow. Rain that falls through a layer of cold air can partly freeze, forming sleet. Alternatively, snow or hail that falls through a warm layer of air will partly melt, also forming sleet.

THUNDER AND LIGHTNING

Thunderstorms form in large cumulonimbus clouds. The cloud particles are blown up and down by violent air currents. As the particles collide and rub together, they become either negatively (–), or positively (+) charged. The pictures below show what happens next.

HOW FORK LIGHTNING OCCURS

Positively charged particles collect at the cloud top, and negatively charged particles collect at the base. The ground below the cloud becomes positively charged.

The attraction between the negative charge at the cloud's base and the ground's positive charge builds until the negative charge is released to the ground in a giant spark, called the leader stroke.

The ground's electrical charge shoots back up to the cloud along the narrow path made by the leader stroke. This second lightning bolt is called the return stroke. It is stronger than the leader stroke.

HEARING THUNDER

The enormous energy of a bolt of lightning heats the air around it by thousands of degrees, causing it to expand suddenly. This makes a giant bang – the sound of thunder.

Light travels at a speed of 300,000km per second, while sound travels at only 350m per second. This is why you hear thunder some time after you see lightning, even though they happen at exactly the same time.

SHEET LIGHTNING

In a thunderstorm, look at the clouds and you will probably see sheet lightning. This is caused by huge electrical sparks inside thunder clouds.

This is fork lightning. Look out for it whenever there is a thunderstorm. Flashes like this are so swift that you barely have time to see them before they are gone.

33

WIND

Warm air rises, creating an area of low pressure on the Earth beneath it. Cool air sinks, creating high pressure on the land or sea below. As warm air rises, cool air moves in to replace it. This movement of air is wind.

The Earth's cold regions (near the Poles) have cold high-pressure air above them. Warmer regions, near the Equator, have warm air above them, so they have low pressure. Air moves between these regions, causing wind.

The movement of air within the Earth's atmosphere

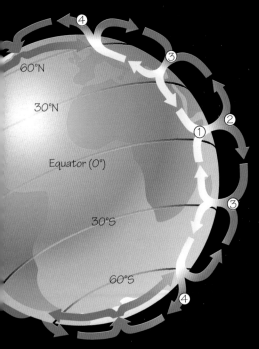

60°N

30°N

Equator (0°)

30°S

60°S

❶ Warm air rising at the Equator produces a band of low pressure.

❷ As this air rises higher in the troposphere, it cools.

❸ The cool air sinks to form bands of high pressure in the areas around 30° north and south of the Equator.

❹ The air in these bands moves to meet the colder, denser air moving away from the Poles, and is forced to rise once more, forming bands of low pressure at around 60° north and south. These are areas of unsettled weather.

THE CORIOLIS EFFECT

If the Earth stood still, winds would keep to a basic north-south pattern. But the Earth spins around, like a top.

The Earth's spin causes its winds to swerve off course. This is called the Coriolis effect.

This diagram shows how wind directions are influenced by the Coriolis effect.

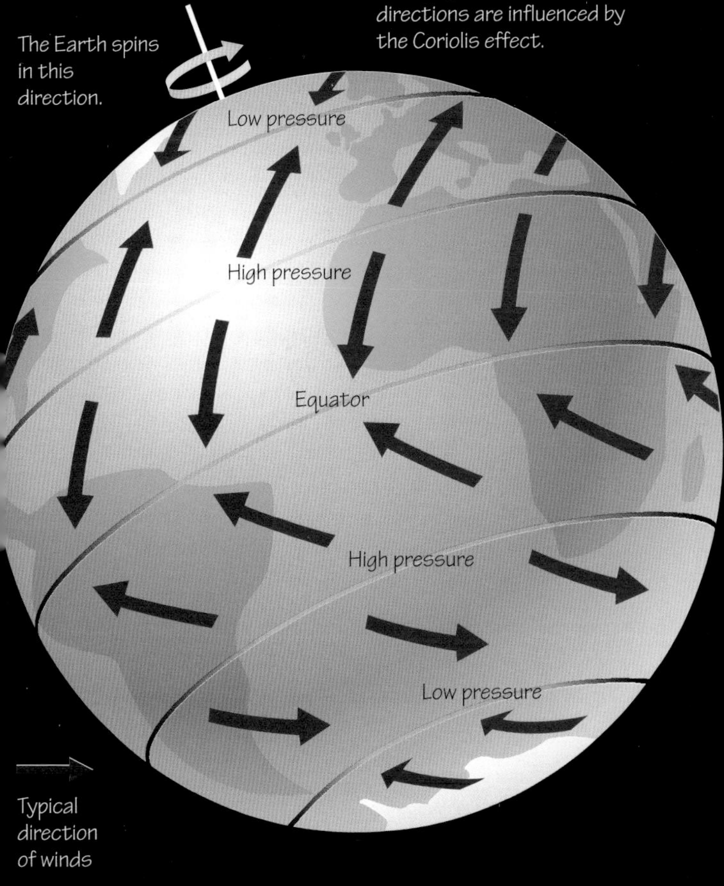

The Earth spins in this direction.

Low pressure

High pressure

Equator

High pressure

Low pressure

Typical direction of winds

WIND AND WEATHER

An area of high or low pressure on the Earth's surface brings particular patterns of wind and weather.

HIGHS...

Areas of high pressure are also called highs, or anticyclones. They bring gentle winds. The weather in a high is fine, warm and settled in summer and very cold but settled in winter. You can find out more about them on page 50.

... AND LOWS

Areas of low pressure are also called lows, cyclones, or depressions. They bring frequently changing winds that can blow very hard. The weather is variable and is usually rainy, too. For more about these, see pages 44-49.

These palm trees are being buffeted by winds created in an area of low pressure. The winds can become so fierce that they knock down the sturdiest of trees, and even flatten buildings.

WIND PATTERNS

Winds spiral away from highs: clockwise in the northern hemisphere and anticlockwise in the southern hemisphere.

Winds spiral in towards lows: anticlockwise in the northern hemisphere and clockwise in the southern hemisphere.

WIND SPEED

Weather forecasters measure wind speed accurately, using specialized equipment. There are many different types. The illustration here shows a device called a cup anemometer.

It records the number of times the shaft turns every minute. This figure is converted to knots, kilometres per hour or miles per hour.

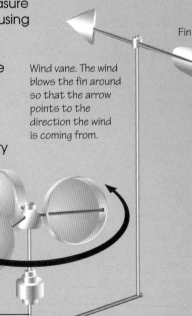

Arrow

Fin

Wind vane. The wind blows the fin around so that the arrow points to the direction the wind is coming from.

The cups catch the wind, and cause the central shaft to spin.

Shaft

37

For a link to a site with virtual hurricanes and twisters, turn to page 61.

LOCAL WINDS

In some regions of the Earth, there are wind patterns which affect the local weather.

LAND-SEA BREEZES

These occur on coasts. During the day, the land heats up faster than the sea. Warm air rising over the land is replaced by a cool, onshore sea breeze.

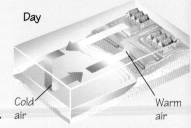

Day

Cold air

Warm air

At night, the land cools faster than the sea. Warm air rising off the sea is replaced by cool air blowing offshore, from the land to the sea.

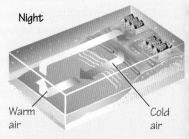

Night

Warm air

Cold air

VALLEY WINDS

Night

Air on slopes cools and sinks

Fog may form

Day

Air on slopes warms and rises

These form in mountain regions on clear nights. At dusk, air on the snowy valley sides cools rapidly. It sinks beneath warmer air in the valleys, causing fog and frost.

In the daytime, sunlight warms the slopes of the valley sides. Air touching the slopes warms rapidly and rises quickly. Winds blow up the sides of the valley.

MONSOONS

These winds occur in India and South-east Asia. They are large-scale, seasonal versions of a land-sea breeze.

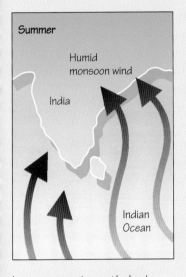

Summer

Humid monsoon wind

India

Indian Ocean

Winter

India

Dry air blows out towards the sea

Indian Ocean

Low-pressure air over the land rises, and is replaced by very humid air (the monsoon wind), which blows in from the sea.

The land is cooler than the sea, so winds blow from the land towards the sea, drying out on the way.

In early June (the hottest month) the difference between low pressure over India and high pressure over the ocean causes a humid monsoon wind to blow. The wind cools as it rises over mountains. Clouds form, and torrential rains fall.

The dry winter winds can make the land arid and barren. If the next summer's wet monsoon winds are late, the crops will die from lack of water. As a result, harvests are poor, which can lead to food shortages.

AIR MASSES

Air masses are huge volumes of air that have uniform temperature and humidity. They are made when a giant portion of air rests over a sea or land mass with a fairly even temperature and humidity. The air takes on the temperature and humidity of the surface.

Air masses are named according to where they form. They are: Arctic (A), the coldest; Polar (P); Tropical (T); Equatorial (E), the warmest. Any air mass formed at sea is described as Maritime (m), and any formed over land is called Continental (c).

This map shows examples of air masses, and how they are named.

Continental Polar
(cP)

Maritime Polar
(mP)

Maritime Tropical
(mT)

Continental Tropical
(cT)

MOVING AIR MASSES

Air is always moving over the Earth's surface. When air masses leave the place where they formed, they alter, getting warmer or cooler, drier or moister, according to the different surfaces they travel over.

Fresh masses of polar and tropical air are produced at the Poles and in the Tropics, so the cycle is always repeated.

POLAR FRONTS

Polar air does not mix with tropical air. Where two meet, a boundary occurs, called a polar front. There is one in each hemisphere. At the boundaries, unsettled weather occurs.

This map shows Polar and Tropical air mass movement, with polar fronts.

■ Maritime Polar   □ Continental Polar   ----- Polar front
■ Maritime Tropical   □ Continental Tropical

JET STREAMS

Where cold and warm air meet in the troposphere, about 10km up from the Earth's surface, sharp differences in air pressure occur. This produces strong winds, called the jet streams. They are shaped like giant squashed tubes which stretch around the globe and are hundreds of kilometres wide.

WHERE ON EARTH

Jet streams weave an uneven path around the Earth. They occur in four places, two in the northern hemisphere, and two in the southern hemisphere. They all blow from west to east, as shown in the picture on the right.

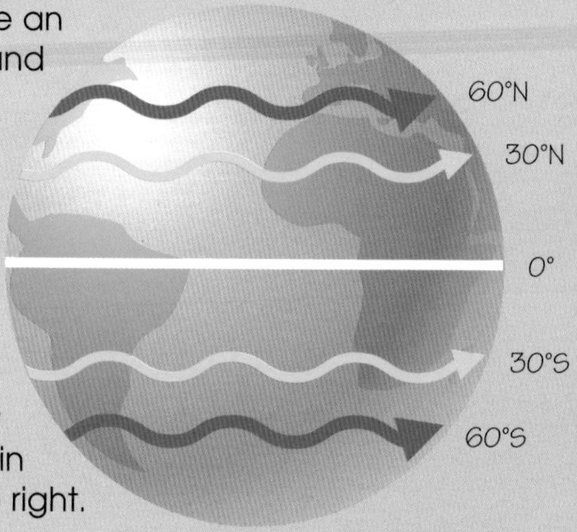

60°N

30°N

0°

30°S

60°S

Polar front jet stream. Average speed: 50–120 kph. Maximum recorded: over 300kph.

Subtropical jet stream. Less powerful than Polar front jet stream.

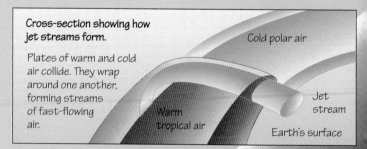

Cross-section showing how jet streams form.

Plates of warm and cold air collide. They wrap around one another, forming streams of fast-flowing air.

Cold polar air

Jet stream

Warm tropical air

Earth's surface

AFFECTING WEATHER

Jet streams disrupt air on either side of their paths. This affects air movement at lower altitudes. They drag highs and lows along, producing high pressure areas within bands of low pressure and vice versa.

The resulting surface air movements produce the everyday winds that we feel just above the Earth's surface. The diagram below shows how a jet stream's movements can influence the weather events beneath it.

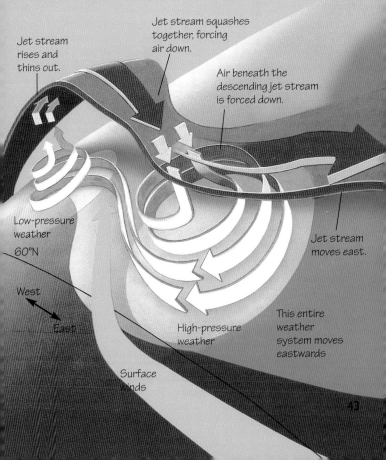

Jet stream squashes together, forcing air down.

Jet stream rises and thins out.

Air beneath the descending jet stream is forced down.

Low-pressure weather 60°N

Jet stream moves east.

West

East

High-pressure weather

This entire weather system moves eastwards

Surface winds

DEPRESSIONS

Listen out for mentions of "depressions" on weather forecasts. These are areas of low atmospheric pressure, which bring rain, storms and changing temperatures.

This map shows the areas of cold and warm air on Earth.

HOW DEPRESSIONS FORM

Depressions form where warm air, which moves away from the Equator, meets cold air, which moves away from the polar regions.

☐ Cold air	☐ Front
☐ Warm air	➤ Wind direction

Occasionally, the warm, moist air bulges into the cool, dry air. The front part of this bulging warm air is called a warm front.

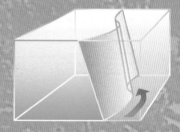

The warm, light air rises over the cold, heavy air. Below the rising air the pressure drops. Cold air rushes in to replace the rising warm air. This is a cold front. It spirals towards the centre of the depression.

● Centre of depression

44

IDENTIFYING A DEPRESSION

From space, depressions are fairly easy to recognize by their distinctive spiral shape. The picture on this page shows a depression over the Atlantic ocean.

Depressions are sometimes called lows, or cyclones.

In the northern hemisphere, depressions spiral in an anticlockwise direction, and move eastwards.

In the southern hemisphere, depressions spiral in a clockwise direction, and move eastwards.

45

FRONTAL WEATHER

If a depression passes over you, the weather will change several times. Clear spells alternate with rain, winds vary in speed and direction, and temperatures fluctuate.

WARM FRONT

As the warm front approaches, cirrus streaks (1) appear, followed by cirrostratus clouds. The air pressure falls. The wind changes direction, getting stronger.

When the front passes over at ground level, clouds thicken into altostratus and nimbostratus (2). Heavy rain or snow falls, and carries on until the front passes.

When the warm front has passed, the air pressure stops falling, the wind changes direction again, and the temperature rises. Cloud breaks up into stratocumulus clouds (3). Light drizzle or snow falls.

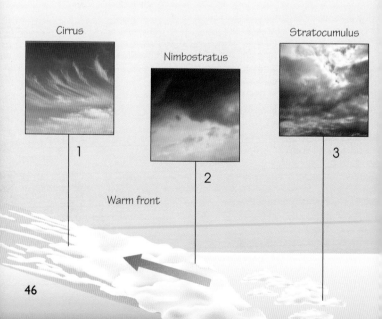

Cirrus

Nimbostratus

Stratocumulus

1

2

3

Warm front

BETWEEN THE FRONTS

Between the two fronts, the weather is calm and mild. Temperature, wind and pressure stabilize. If the sun is strong, clouds dry out. Otherwise it stays overcast.

As the cold front approaches, the wind changes direction, becoming gusty. Pressure falls, but the temperature stays steady. Cumulus clouds form (4).

COLD FRONT

As the front arrives, a solid bank of cumulus, altostratus and cumulonimbus clouds advances, bringing heavy showers of rain or snow (5). There may even be thunder or hail showers.

When the front passes at ground level, temperatures fall, but pressure rises and visibility improves. The sky clears, with fewer clouds, and one or two showers (6).

Cumulonimbus

Cumulus humilis

Cumulus

5

Cold front

6

4

OCCLUDED FRONTS

If the cold front of a depression catches up with the warm front, they merge in a single front, called an occlusion. Here is a description of what happens.

☐ Cold air
☐ Warm air
☐ Front
↘ Wind direction

The cold front sweeps around. It starts to catch up with the warm front. The warm sector gets squeezed. Eventually, the cold front touches the warm front.

The warm sector is lifted up away from the Earth's surface. The warm sector becomes a pool of warm air, which rests on top of the cold polar air.

The cold air lifts the warm air higher. As it rises, the warm air cools, causing the water vapour that it carries to condense. This results in huge clouds and heavy rain. After the rain, the depression dies out.

WEATHER MAPS

Look out for TV weather maps showing depressions. They show fronts and maybe air pressure details. Air pressure on the Earth's surface is indicated by a system of numbered lines, called isobars. These join places with the same air pressure. Depressions are centred in the middle of the isobar with the lowest number.

FRONTAL SYMBOLS

Depressions are indicated by symbols, as in the weather map on the right. These symbols are explained below.

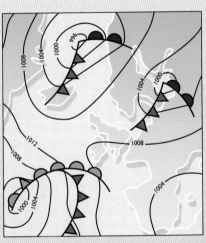

This map shows depressions over the north Atlantic and Europe.

Key	
Warm front	●●●●●●
Cold front	▲▲▲▲▲
Occlusion	●▲●▲●
Isobars	1004

ISOBARS

Places along the line of an isobar have the same pressure. The figure written next to an isobar, which indicates its pressure, is always expressed in millibars. 1,000 millibars is about the same as 2kg pressing down on every square centimetre of the Earth's surface.

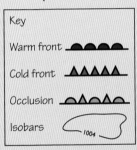

49

ANTICYCLONES

Anticyclones are areas of high pressure, sometimes called highs. They tend to form at high altitudes. The air in anticyclones sinks, becoming warm and dry. As this happens, clouds disappear. Highs move slowly and bring little wind or rain; the weather is usually settled.

HIGHS IN SUMMER

The ground and the air near the Earth's surface are warm and dry, so anticyclones tend to create hot, sunny days and blue skies.

Day: temperatures rise quickly in the hot sunshine. Dew and mist evaporate swiftly.

Night: clear skies allow ground heat to radiate quickly – temperatures drop rapidly. Dew and mist form.

In summer, high pressure weather tends to be clear, dry, settled and warm.

HIGHS IN WINTER

The ground and the air near the surface are cold. Clear blue skies and sunny weather can result. Warmth radiates away quickly, so temperatures stay low.

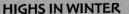 Day: temperatures rise very slowly in the weak winter sunshine.

Night: Earth's heat is lost quickly into the clear sky. Air temperatures fall and fog and frost form.

STAYING OVERCAST

Because the winter sunshine is so feeble, on some days the temperature just doesn't get high enough for foggy, overcast weather to clear. Instead, it stays gloomy, still and chilly all day long.

TROPICAL STORMS

Tropical storms take place in the seas near the Equator. They develop from depressions during the hottest time of the year – summer and early autumn. At this time, the seas are very warm.

■ The red areas on this map show where tropical storms occur frequently.

HOW THEY FORM

As the air above the warm seas is heated, it becomes very humid. It rises quickly, creating very low pressure below, near the sea. Winds rush into this low-pressure area and whirl upwards. As they rise, they cool, forming clouds.

Huge amounts of water vapour condense out from the humid, rising air to form towering cumulonimbus and cumulus clouds. A huge, spiralling storm results, with giant clouds and driving rain. At the centre is a calm core, called the "eye", which is about 40km across.

Air cools as it rises. Walls of cloud form.

Winds rush in

Low pressure

Warm sea

Eye of the storm

Strong winds

DESTRUCTIVE POWER

The strongest, most destructive tropical storms are named according to where in the world they originate:

- Around India – cyclone;
- Asia/Australia – typhoon;
- Caribbean – hurricane.

Tropical storms can cause huge destruction. This photo shows some of the damage done to the city of Darwin, Australia, by a typhoon. 90% of the city was devastated.

TORNADOES

Tornadoes are violent, twisting, funnel-shaped winds that can extend downwards from the base of cumulonimbus clouds. They are also known as twisters.

HOW THEY FORM

Tornadoes form in summer-time, in humid air where winds blow into each other from opposite directions. They happen over land, not water, and are accompanied by heavy rain, thunder and lightning. They form mainly in North America, but are less common elsewhere.

WHAT THEY DO

The pressure inside a tornado is so high that it can rip apart things that it touches, such as buildings. A very strong updraught of air is created, too, which sucks up everything in its path.

This tornado is ripping through Oklahoma, USA. Weather forecasters track tornadoes, using radars and satellites. They pass on tornado warnings to the public.

...AND LOOKALIKES

WATERSPOUTS
Waterspouts are formed over lakes and seas, mainly in the tropics. Many occur when tornadoes pass over water. Some water is lifted as spray, but most of the waterspout consists of cloud droplets.

FUNNEL CLOUDS
These are mini-versions of tornadoes and waterspouts. They can be seen in all parts of the world.

DUST DEVILS
These are confined to hot desert areas. They grow up from the ground, not down from clouds. Spirals of warm air rise off the baked earth, sweeping up dust and debris. They last for just a few minutes.

WEATHER SATELLITES

Weather forecasters use satellites up in space to help them predict weather conditions.

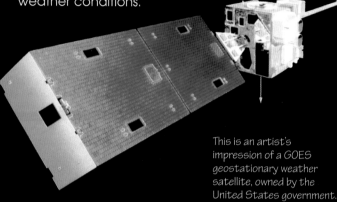

This is an artist's impression of a GOES geostationary weather satellite, owned by the United States government.

There are two main types of weather satellite.

• Geostationary satellites stay in one position over the Earth. They do this by orbiting at the same speed as Earth's rotation.

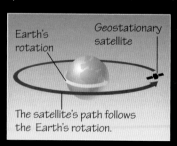

Earth's rotation

Geostationary satellite

The satellite's path follows the Earth's rotation.

These observe and predict short-term general weather patterns.

• Polar-orbiting satellites go around and around the Earth from Pole to Pole. They shift slightly westward on each orbit.

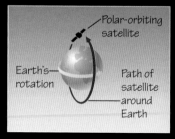

Polar-orbiting satellite

Earth's rotation

Path of satellite around Earth

These orbit close to the Earth, so they record detailed information.

For a link to a site where you can track satellites in 3D, turn to page 61.

DATA COLLECTION

Modern satellites are packed with equipment that gathers accurate information about Planet Earth and its weather.

• Imaging devices show the amount of light or heat that is coming from the Earth. They observe clouds and temperatures.

In this image of the USA, the very lightest grey areas are blankets of cloud.

• Signals are bounced off the Earth, to find out about temperature and moisture levels in the atmosphere.

• Data processors collect and analyse information sent up from weather-recording equipment on Earth.

This digital image was put together from data recorded by a satellite. It shows lots of information about the Earth. For example, the red and purple areas are heavy rainclouds. The yellow areas on the land are desert regions. The grey patches are high-level clouds.

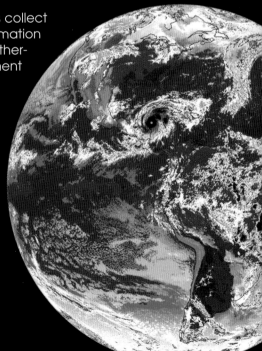

WEATHER FORECASTING

Weather forecasts are compiled by meteorologists. They interpret data provided by weather stations, ships, aircraft, weather balloons, satellites and radars. Then they publish the information in a standardized form – a synoptic chart, like the one shown here.

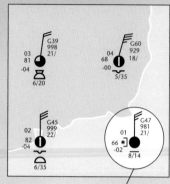

This picture shows part of a synoptic chart

SYNOPTIC CHART SYMBOLS

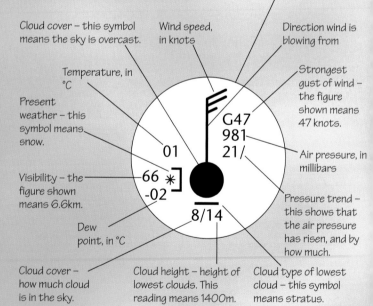

Cloud cover – this symbol means the sky is overcast.

Wind speed, in knots

Direction wind is blowing from

Temperature, in °C

Present weather – this symbol means snow.

Strongest gust of wind – the figure shown means 47 knots.

Air pressure, in millibars

Visibility – the figure shown means 6.6km.

Dew point, in °C

Pressure trend – this shows that the air pressure has risen, and by how much.

Cloud cover – how much cloud is in the sky.

Cloud height – height of lowest clouds. This reading means 1400m.

Cloud type of lowest cloud – this symbol means stratus.

WEATHER SYMBOLS

Meteorologists plot their recordings of weather conditions in the exact places where the recording was made. The complicated array of symbols that they use is explained below.

Present weather symbols

=	Mist	△	Hail
≡	Fog	℞	Thunder storm
⁹	Drizzle	▽	Shower
•	Rain	✳ ▽	Snow shower
∴	Continuous moderate rain	]	Observation in previous hour
∴	Continuous heavy rain		
✳	Snow		

Cloud cover symbols

Show how many "oktas" (eighths) of the sky are covered by cloud

○	Clear sky		6 oktas
	1 okta		7 oktas
	2 oktas	●	Overcast
	3 oktas	⊖	No record
	4 oktas	⊗	Sky obscured (e.g. by fog)
	5 oktas		

Cloud type symbols

⌣	Cirrus (Ci)
⌇	Cirrocumulus (Cc)
ꝛ	Cirrostratus (Cs)
∠	Altostratus (As)
⌣	Altocumulus (Ac)
⫽	Nimbostratus (Ns)
—	Stratus (S)
⌐⌣	Stratocumulus (Sc)
⌒	Cumulus (Cu)
☒	Cumulonimbus (Cb)

Wind speed symbols

Knots

0	⊙	23-27	\\\\—○
1-2	—○	28-32	\\\\—○
3-7	⌐—○	33-37	\\\\\—○
8-12	⌐—○	38-42	\\\\\—○
13-17	\\—○	43-47	\\\\\\—○
18-22	\\\—○	48-52	▲—○

For a link to a site about how weather forecasters work, turn to page 61.

WEATHER MAP

This is the type of weather map that you see on television. It uses a simple style, so you can follow the weather at a glance. Maps like this are made by forecasters using information from synoptic charts.

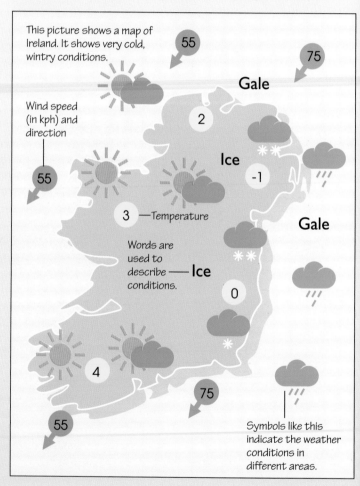

This picture shows a map of Ireland. It shows very cold, wintry conditions.

Wind speed (in kph) and direction

55

Gale

75

2

Ice

-1

3 —Temperature

Words are used to describe conditions.

Ice

0

Gale

4

75

55

Symbols like this indicate the weather conditions in different areas.

INTERNET LINKS

If you have access to the Internet, you can visit these websites to find out more about weather. For links to these sites, go to the Usborne Quicklinks Website at **www.usborne-quicklinks.com** and enter the keywords "spotters weather".

Internet safety

When using the Internet, please follow the **Internet safety guidelines** shown on the Usborne Quicklinks Website.

WEBSITE 1 Get up-to-date weather forecasts for over 5,000 different places around the world.

WEBSITE 2 Weather news, forecasts and satellite imagery from the UK Meteorological Office.

WEBSITE 3 The website of the US National Weather Service.

WEBSITE 4 Detailed guide to meteorology, with maps, diagrams and activities.

WEBSITE 5 See worldwide weather and climate data, and find out about how weather forecasters work.

WEBSITE 6 An online guide to weather, with explanations and photos.

WEBSITE 7 All about clouds and how to identify them.

WEBSITE 8 Track weather satellites around the world in live 3D.

WEBSITE 9 Create virtual hurricanes and twisters, then explore case studies of real ones.

WEBSITE 10 Satellite images of recent major weather events.

USEFUL WORDS

accretion - the freezing together of ice particles and crystals in clouds, forming snow or hail.

anticyclone - an area of high atmospheric pressure.

barometer - an instrument for measuring air pressure.

coalescence - the process by which raindrops form, as water droplets collide and join together in clouds.

condensation - when water vapour (a gas) becomes liquid water.

cyclone - see *depression*.

depression - an area of low atmospheric pressure.

dew point - the temperature at which water vapour condenses from the air.

evaporation - when a liquid changes into a vapour.

front - where two different air masses meet.

humidity - the amount of water vapour held in the air.

hygrometer - an instrument for measuring the air's humidity.

infrared (IR) radiation - heat energy from the Sun.

knot - a unit of wind speed, equivalent to 1.85kph.

meteorology - the scientific study of the weather.

nimbus - a rain cloud.

ozone - a gas which forms a layer in the atmosphere, protecting the Earth from ultraviolet radiation.

precipitation - water falling from the sky in any form: rain, sleet, snow or hail.

sublimation - changing from solid to gas without first becoming liquid.

supercooled - a liquid that is colder than freezing but has not become solid.

surface wind - a wind that blows near the Earth's surface.

tropical storm - a powerful storm that forms in the seas near the Equator at the hottest time of year.

tropopause - the boundary between the troposphere and the stratosphere.

ultraviolet (UV) radiation - Short wavelength energy from the Sun. It is harmful.

INDEX